Bibliographic information published by the German National Library:

The German National Library lists this publication in the National Bibliography; detailed bibliographic data are available on the Internet at http://dnb.dnb.de .

Imprint:

Copyright © 2018 GRIN Verlag
Print and binding: Books on Demand GmbH, Norderstedt Germany
ISBN: 9783346012944

Felipe-Jordi Rahn Bueno

Chinese FDI Regulation. Development and Benefit for the Chinese Economy

GRIN Verlag

GRIN - Your knowledge has value

Since its foundation in 1998, GRIN has specialized in publishing academic texts by students, college teachers and other academics as e-book and printed book. The website www.grin.com is an ideal platform for presenting term papers, final papers, scientific essays, dissertations and specialist books.

Essay on

The development of Chinese FDI regulation and how it was beneficial for the Chinese economy

Freie Universität Berlin Fall Semester 17/18: Multinational Enterprises (MNEs), Investment Policy and Sustainable Development

Name: Felipe-Jordi Rahn Bueno

Introduction

My paper will address the development of the Chinese economy and in which way the regulation of foreign direct investment (FDI) helped China to overcome a financial trough and to swing themselves up to one of the biggest players on the global market. Therefore, my guiding question will be "How has the Chinese regulation of FDI from the late 1970s until the 2000s boosted the economy of the country?". My topic and research question are relevant because the economic evolution China has been through is unique, even though its growth model was like those of other Asian or Communist countries and other states like the UDSSR failed to transition their market into a more liberal system. The astonishing success story that China has written was greatly influenced by the opening to FDI whilst still having restrictions on it to channel it into the right sectors for developing the country. This essay is based on the neoclassical growth theory which seems to fit the most since the three driving factors of this theory are labour, capital and technology, which are all important factors of China´s economic growth. To explain its case, I will mainly use academic literature from researchers specialized on Chinese economy, a scientific article and a study. I will use data from the Worldbank and from various surveys that Long (2005) evaluated to point out and underline the growth of China´s economy. I found that FDI clearly helped to spur the rise of the Chinese economy, even though the study of Ford (2010) did not find direct benefits of FDI in China in the long run but admits positive indirect effects. My findings in this paper are therefore that the applied regulative measures were effective at the time but might not be sustainable if they wanted to use this set of regulations in the future.

China´s Problematic Situation

Until the late 1970s China was a country with almost no trade and a very low GDP – not just per capita but in total - compared to developed states.

To understand how crucial the regulation policy on FDI by the Chinese government in terms of promoting economic growth was, it is necessary to understand the situation of China before their tremendous growth, because it was not a lack of financial resources that hindered the Chinese economy to grow but rather the low technological standard and trade policy in the country. Before the liberalization of the Chinese economy it was very similar to the system of the UdSSR and a demand-economy in which only twelve state-owned companies controlled the foreign trade and had monopolies on it (Naughton, 2006). China imported to decrease shortages or to access products they could not produce and most importantly technology. But this was, in fact, a problem since the Chinese currency was set arbitrarily and was by far

1

overvalued until 1986 when reformers made it possible to sell the above plan foreign currency earnings on a secondary market and a more realistic value was adopted. The overvaluation made it difficult to export and generate foreign exchange. For companies that were not a state-owned foreign trade company as well as for natural persons it was also nearly impossible to get the permission to exchange the Chinese Renminbi. China soon lacked foreign currency to pay for their imports and foreign technology like production machines. Therefore, they had to adjust their strategy to generate the foreign exchange to cover their expenses.

The Liberalization Process

Export Processing Contracts

They decided to gradually approach the liberalization of their economy. The main goal was to bring foreign currency into the country and the government's depots but without letting foreign firms into the domestic market because that would have led to an interference of world market prices with the planned prices of the Chinese 5-year-plan system. That would have in consequence caused problems for the state-owned industry that benefitted from the Chinese socialist price system and from which the government harvested most of its budget. The only way to achieve this main goal would be to encourage exports – which were until 1979 mostly just seen as a means to pay for imports but were not very popular in the demand economy of China.

Consequently, due to the lack of foreign currency to import advanced technology and thereby expedite the industrial progress of the country the Chinese system had to open to cross-border trade. To gain access to foreign exchange through foreign trade the government decided to allow export-processing in 1978. Foreign companies (especially from Hong Kong) could use the manpower of the PRC to manufacture their goods in mainland China whilst always owning them. In that way the restrictive legislation on imports could be overcome. The Chinese manufacturers would earn a fee and the finished product would not be taxed due to the special regulations (Naughton, 2006).

Opening the Door to Foreign Business

The first step of legislation in favour of FDI was the law of the People's Republic of China on joint ventures using Chinese and foreign investment in July 1979, which opened the door for foreign investors with the restriction to form a joint venture to enter the Chinese market, in that the foreign investor does not own more than 50 percent of the shares (Ford, 2010). But the country's decision makers were afraid to make mistakes during the establishment of another trading system and that the home-based economy would be put under pressure through the possibility of FDI and the engagement in companies.

Therefore, they decided to erect a variety of tariff and non-tariff barriers as they slowly dismantled their planned trading system. Firstly, they put up high tariffs to protect the domestic market. Long (2005) states an average tariff level of 55,6 percent in 1982 which would stay high but decline slowly in the next decade. In 1992 the Worldbank found the unweighted mean tariff to be at 43 percent and the trade-weighted tariff at 32 percent in China. According to Naughton (2006) those numbers were not unusual for protective developing countries, even though it seemed odd for a country that put so much effort into appearing as a state that makes its way into a liberal system. Secondly, China worked with a set of non-tariff barriers such as the limitation of trading rights which still belonged mainly to the state-owned foreign-trade companies. Those were as well the only ones who were granted the right to import for the domestic market and therefore had access to it. Export-processing manufactures were only granted exceptional rights for imports but were restricted to goods needed for production and kept from sensitive goods like fertilizer or staple foods. (Naughton, 2006)

Taxation System and Exemptions

For direction and protection measures China used various taxes to lead FDI to the place where it was needed to gain the benefits the government wanted from letting it in. Companies had to pay corporate income tax as well as tariffs and since 1994 a 17 percent value added tax (VAT). For specific sectors of the economy like the automobile industry there was an excise tax of ten percent. This would decrease the profits of export production of foreign companies drastically in comparison to production at home which is why China used a tactic of exemptions and reimbursements for export manufacturers. If producers imported materials for the means of reexporting, they were exempt from VAT and were reimbursed the 17 percent (Long, 2005). Therefore, export producers had an incentive to rather import raw materials for their production instead of being in a competition with domestic producers. If the imports were used to produce for the Chinese market, the full amount of taxes and tariffs had to be paid. Further tax exemptions for foreign investors will be found in the section "The Introduction of Advanced technology".

Special Economic Zones Attract Foreign Business

Simultaneously they started to open Special Economic Zones (SEZ) near Hong Kong and Taiwan, two states that were far more advanced in the development of foreign trade, in 1978. Those SEZs were used as a pilot project for trade, where the restrictions on foreign investment and business were less strict. The SEZs were set in areas, whose economy was even trailing behind the rest of China, so that this project could not do much damage to the provinces. The local governments in the SEZs were granted rights for experimental incentive setting to attract foreign firms and investments. The administrative barriers in those zones were lower and it took less time to open a business there because of a simplified registration. The government specifically encouraged the establishing of Chinese-foreign joint ventures and foreign investment (Naughton, 2006; Kroeber 2016).

Local and central governments profited from the SEZs as the local administrations just had to deliver a certain amount of foreign currency to the central government which was agreed upon in contracts. Everything above that amount the local governments could keep and reinvest. To attract foreign businesses to the SEZs companies were given tax rebates or even tax holidays for the starting years as well as duty-free import rights on goods meant for export production (Naughton, 2006)

This was one of the most important legislative steps. By steering foreign businesses to produce in China for export, the foreign exchange and technology was lured into the country as the domestic market and firms stayed protected against competition from abroad.

Kroeber (2016) found that another beneficial factor of the newly established zones was their location. The small distance to Hong Kong brought also administrative expertise as it was already a big trading hub. Taiwan even moved its already very developed electronic industry to the People´s Republic in the late 1990s what is known as the "Taiwan factor". This should turn out as a huge bonus for the Chinese economy that went on to account for over 40 percent of global exports of electronics nowadays even though it accounted for only about 5 percent in 2000.

Besides technology, foreign invested enterprises brought another major advantage into the country: training. Long (2005) showed that 85,4 percent trained their employees in China and over 20 percent even trained them abroad. Only 8,89 percent of the companies involved in export processing did not train their staff at all. This training does not only benefit the firms who train their staff but also the entire country since most workers do not spend their whole lifetime at one firm. So, when they leave the company that trained them for a domestic one or start their own business, the Chinese economy benefits from their expertise. In Kroeber (2016) it is also argued that the home-based firms were able to learn from the foreign production and management techniques.

Bilateral Investment Treaties Guarantee Protection

Further steps were taken in 1982/83 when they started to implement more legislation on FDI and to conclude their first wave of bilateral investment treaties (BITs) to promote their trade.

The negotiating of BITs was crucial in attracting foreign companies since the trust in the Chinese government was not very high and lots of companies feared to invest because they were concerned that their assets in the country could soon be seized. Therefore, in the BITs China and their first two contracting partner states, Sweden and Germany, agreed on e.g. expropriation protection – companies could not be expropriated without proper legal protocol and compensation. Furthermore, a dispute settlement proceeding was set. In addition to the protection the treaties guaranteed investors the transfer of their funds and equal treatment in comparison to domestic investors or from countries with similar treaties, which is known as most favourable nation agreement (BITs with Sweden, 1982 and Germany ,1983).

According to Naughton (2006) with the implementation of the more liberal policy FDI and GDP rose in the early 1980s but not extraordinarily quick. But especially the former did not rise fast enough, what led the Chinese policymakers to the decision to allow wholly owned subsidiaries in 1986 to push the introduction of more advanced technology forward since foreign companies were not eager to share their intellectual property with possible Chinese business partners. This policy change should pay because beginning in the 1990s the Chinese economy and the FDI inflow started to boom. The FDI inflow rose from around 3,5 bn US$ in 1990 to nearly 42,1 bn US$ in 2000. In the same time the GDP of the PRC mounted from roughly 361 bn US$ to 1,21 tn US$, as Worldbank data shows. Furthermore, policymakers found the export processing experiment in the regions like Guangdong successful and approved contracts of this kind of business in the coastal regions as well in 1986.

The Introduction of Advanced Technology

To advance their technological level China not only tried to import advanced technological innovation via FDI but encouraged the foreign invested companies to let the innovations happen in China. Hence, it was encouraged to establish research and development (R&D) centres in the country. There were various incentives for this like the tax- and tariff-free import of equipment and technology that a company would like to use in product development as well as sales tax-free transfer of technology that a foreign invested company invented. They could even gain a short-time access to the local (therefore domestic) market for products the R&D centre developed to test them. Furthermore, companies were encouraged to raise their research expenses on a yearly basis since a company that upped their R&D expenses in the country by at least ten percent gained a corporate income tax cut on their technological development spending by 50% for the year with higher expenses.

In addition to the R&D centres the foreign invested companies were able to fill technological gaps in China via their own equipment, as Long (2005) found that in 2002 65 percent of the surveyed foreign invested companies adopted technology that was not available in China at that time and 35 percent used the advanced Chinese technology. As Long (2005) goes on, one can see from another survey that 81 percent of all FDI projects in the Chinese capital city added more developed technology which helped push the city´s technological level forward an estimated 15 years. Based on a survey by Jiang which I found in Long (2005) 91,4 percent of foreign invested enterprises registered technological advancement in some kind.

The high level of technology can also be seen in its share of exports as foreign invested enterprises are the main exporters of high technology with a share of more than 75 percent since the beginning of the millennium (Kroeber 2016).

China´s Entry into the World Trade Organization (WTO)

With the application for a WTO membership and the following entry China had to dismantle many barriers and restrictive policy on FDI to be in accordance with different treaties like the TRIMs. As Long (2005) found China abandoned their performance requirements for wholly-owned subsidiaries but continued to encourage exports and the addition of advanced technology. Furthermore, according to the requirements to enter the WTO they started to lower the tariffs about a decade before they were admitted into the organization. As can be found in Naughton (2006) China lowered the average nominal tariff from 43 percent in 1992 to 17 percent in 1999 before they agreed to reduce industrial tariffs to an average of 9,4 percent to join. They also agreed to reduce the agricultural tariffs to 15 percent. Both goals were achieved without any problems.

With the admission to the WTO China also had to change their Guiding Directory and let go of their performance requirements like export proportion, foreign exchange balance, technology transfer and R&D centres (Long, 2005), but kept on encouraging via incentives.

Consistent with the TRIMs they kept their neutral and voluntary policies, e.g. large corporate tax cuts for companies which export at least 70 percent of their production or VAT and tariff exemptions for imports that are used for export processing (Long, 2005). With the entry into the WTO, according to Long (2005) China had to lose different restrictions and the 10 percent excise tax in the automobile sector which was at the time not very innovative since the high barriers protected established companies from competition, said Naughton (2006). With the dismantling of the barriers the price for cars declined while the innovation, productivity and demand rose.

After the WTO entry China experienced a new surge in exports – rising around 27 percent per year in the span from 2001 to 2008 – owing to the easier access to foreign markets around the world through the membership (Kroeber, 2016).

Conclusion

Regarding the neoclassical growth theory China clearly had the labour force that is necessary for economic growth, but they were lacking the technology to promote it. Domestic capital was not the problem either but due to their closed system they were not in possession of enough foreign exchange to buy technology from advanced countries. The course of the Chinese government gave China access to the needed foreign currency and in addition the possibility to enjoy certain technological spillover effects that are inherent with the inflow of FDI. This was clearly one of the major influences FDI had on China since Chinese technology lagged behind the world standard and is the major point in which Long (2005), Naughton (2006) and Kroeber (2016) agree and only Ford (2010) disagrees – probably because the empirical study reduced the factors to logarithms and did not respect the fact that without the opening none of the inflows would have been possible. Ford (2010) on the other hand found the biggest benefit to be the creation of jobs by foreign invested enterprises but Long (2005) sees a problem in the long run since those companies would be able to attract the best Chinese students who then would not work for domestic firms. This leads to another bonus of FDI inflows. The improvement of the human capital through training that is needed to handle high-technology equipment which were brought into the country together with the expertise of foreign invested enterprises. When more and better training is available in the country that leads to a better educated people which then benefits the whole country. I do though agree

7

with Ford (2010) that the impact on FDI on China will not be sustainable but rather harmful if it would be continuously treated exceptionally since China has now reached a point where its technology is on a competitive level and domestic investment would be crowded out by the foreign investment which would in consequence slow down the Chinese economy. Furthermore, Ford (2010) argued that the additional financial capital from foreign investors would not have been needed for economic growth since the domestic capital would have been very productive, whilst Morrison (2018) saw the two capital sources to go "hand in hand" (p.6) and that the economic reforms were the reason for improved efficiency and therefore, increased output. Referring to the neoclassical growth theory I see Ford (2010) in so far in the wrong that the equilibrium of labour, technology and capital was not given before the opening to FDI since labour and (domestic) capital were given but the technology was not developed enough, and advanced technology was only accessible through FDI. Today China is one of the biggest consumer markets and leading in manufacturing and in the discussion of the world´s largest economic power (Morrison, 2018).

However, regarding the research question it was the right way to promote the economic growth in China and to lead it into a technological developed era whilst the restrictions by the government kept fatal competition away from domestic producers. The booming economy even spilled over into the housing industry which can be seen in the enormous surge in steel and cement production (Kroeber 2016). According to Morrison (2018) China´s quick growth since the opening to FDI raised several hundred million people out of poverty.

Bibliography (listed by importance for this essay)

Barry Naughton (2006): The Chinese Economy: Transitions and Growth, MIT Press, Cambridge (Massachusetts)

Moran, Theodore H.; Graham, Edward M.; Blomström, Magnus, u.a. (2005): Does foreign direct investment promote development?, Peterson Institute, Washington, DC, p. 315-336 (Article: China's policies on FDI: review and evaluation by Guoqiang Long)

Arthur Kroeber (2016): China's Economy: What everyone needs to know, Oxford University Press, Oxford

J. L. Ford , S. Sen, Hongxu Wei (2010): FDI and Economic Development in China 1970-2006: A Cointegration study

Morrison, W. M. (2014). China's economic rise: History, trends, challenges, and implications for the United States. Washington, DC: Congressional Research Service.

Bilateral Investment Treaties:

Abkommen zwischen der Bundesrepublik Deutschland und der Volksrepublik China über die Forderung und den gegenseitigen Schutz von Kapitalanlagen, 1983

Agreement on the Mutual Protection of Investment Between the Government of the Kingdom of Sweden and the Government of the People's Republic of China, 1982